MW01030000

ARISE

Spiritual Formation for the Apostolic Reformation

ROB COVELL

ARISE

Spiritual Formation for the Apostolic Reformation

ROB COVELL

Arise: Spiritual Formation
for the Apostolic Reformation
Rob Covell

© Printed 2020

ISBN -13: 978-0-9986539-4-5

Quest Theological Institute

A Division of Quiver Full Publishing

Cover and inside design layout
Carolyn Covell

Printed in the USA

INTRODUCTION

We live in one the most exciting times in Christian history. Many of us in the Body of Christ can sense things are changing in our times but we do not have language for what we are experiencing. *Arise* is written to help us understand the times and seasons we are living in, and to strengthen God's Global Church as she experiences one of the most exciting times in Church History: the return of Apostolic Government of the Church and the rapid expansion of Christianity across the world. Apostolic Theologian, Dr. C. Peter Wagner, identified this movement in the 1990's, and today many Christians are experiencing the graces of God and the goodness of God in their lives through this reformation. In fact, almost every Christian denomination has been influenced by the New Apostolic Reformation.

Christian demographers and sociologists have been seeing the shift in Christianity for two decades as they have observed the rise of Apostolic Networks, rapid church growth, prophetic ministry, signs and wonders, powerful worship movements and the emergence of a modern Christianity that is empowered to heal society and culture. It begs to ask the question: what are the reasons for these major shifts in modern Christianity? What are the belief systems that empower these dynamic changes the Apostolic Reformation is bringing to Christianity, and how do Christians accelerate this reformation? *Arise* is written to answer these questions and empower leaders within the Apostolic Reformation to identify these distinctives so that the Apostolic Reformation coalesces and matures. *Arise* is a tool to build God's people and release them into their Kingdom destinies.

Frui itinere – enjoy the journey!

- Rob Covell

ACKNOWLEDGEMENTS

I want to acknowledge the following men and women who have given me vision for this project and have influenced the way I think about our faith: Dr. Che Ahn, Tony Kim, David Collins, Johnny and Elizabeth Enlow, Dr. Harold Eberle, Benny Yang, Dr. Greg Wallace, Yvonne Camper, Jeremy Nelson and Miranda Nelson. I appreciate all you do for the Body of Christ. You have all imparted graces and gifts in my life. Blessings!

THANKSGIVING

I want to thank my wife Carolyn who always encourages me and loves me. She is my Jesus-with-skin-on and the most beautiful person in the world. I want to thank The Refuge Community for being amazing Spirit-filled people who love God. You are bold, free and passion-ate for Christ. You are amazing people who love well and will change the world. I want to thank David Collins for being my spiritual father and for loving me with Jesus' love, helping me mature as a leader. I want to thank my staff at The Refuge Community. You are all amazing people who are called to accomplish great things for God.

CONTENTS

Chapter One

CALLED TO CO-LABOR WITH GOD

The theological battle of our day is centered on our perception of God. What we think and believe about God shapes the way we live and the choices we make. The accumulative effect of our thoughts about God over our lifetimes ultimately determine our destiny in this life, and the one to come. So, it is important that our understanding and knowledge of God accurately reflects His heart. Even the quality of our lives in the present, and over the course of our lifetimes, are affected by what we know to be true about the Lord. In John 10:10, Jesus said, "I have come that they will have life and have it abundantly." He said this in contrast to the mission of the thief - or the devil - which is to kill, steal and destroy. I mention this because oftentimes God is blamed for the kill, steal, and destroy stuff that we encounter in the various seasons of our lives. We say things like, "I guess it is God's will that I am suffering in my health." Or we'll say something like, "I guess it is God's will for me to struggle financially," and many other "I guess" statements that we all have said from time to time when we encounter a situation contrary to the goodness of God. These types of statements reveal our hearts are believing lies about God regarding the specific need we have at that time. But what if we could live in a way where the experiential knowledge of God, the truth of His words and our faith collide, giving us a better reality than the one we are experiencing?

The creation account in Genesis Chapters 1 and 2 introduce us to an awesome, powerful and loving God who created us with kind intentions and a divine destiny. The Lord God spoke the heavens, the earth, the plants and the animals into existence. But when God created humanity, He formed him with His hands. This shows us that God intimately touched humanity, using supernatural loving hands to form those made in His image and likeness. This truth is the foundation for living in the love of God.

Let's explore what was on God's mind when He made people in His image

and likeness. This will help us to be transformed by the renewing of our minds.
This is the first step for reordering our
perception of God which will empower
a God-colored perception of ourselves
and the people around us.

The best way to unpack the
Scriptures in a way that will help us see
the Lord's heart is to understand the
meaning of the words we are reading in
their original languages. Genesis 1:26-28
tells us that people were made in God's
image and in His likeness. It also goes on
to say He blessed them, giving them the
prosperity and the grace to accomplish
their mandate to be fruitful, to multiply,
and to rule. These two verses reveal deep
theological truths which will help us walk
in the blessing, favor, and confidence in
God's love for us, enabling us to extend
that love and grace to others.

The Hebrew word for "image" is
tselem, which means resemblance. Just
as God possesses wisdom, knowledge,
creativity, power, glory, love, grace, and
purity, we too bear these qualities as ones
who resemble God, albeit limited. The
realization of being made in His image

imputes intrinsic value on humanity. This is foundational to understanding that humanity was worth saving from God's point of view. God had in mind for mankind to reflect Himself as humanity expressed itself from the beginning of creation until eternity. Even in our fallen state, we still reflect His image. It is a damaged image, but one that is being restored to Eden by God's very own narrative of salvation in Jesus Christ. God the Father is committed to His original design and intent for us. You could say He relates to us in destiny, and in the long-term care of each one of us as we walk out our life paths.

The Hebrew word for "likeness" is dĕmuwth, which means similitude. This word implies that we are an expression of the One we are made like. Most English dictionaries define this word as likeness; expression of; or an allegory. How awesome it is to know that each one of us is a unique expression of the One who created us! Humanity, being an allegory, is a shocking statement because an allegory communicates deep spiritual insight in an easy to see story. Jesus used allegories all throughout His teachings, taking everyday examples of life and using them to communicate deep spiritual truth about Himself, the Father and Holy Spirit. What is being communicated to us is that as we observe the lives of people, they become an allegory of God's story because we see God in them.

As we consider all these things, we can conclude the Lord God had a very high and purely positive view of people. As we consider these truths and apply them personally, suddenly we become aware that God has always had genuinely kind and loving intentions for us and all of humanity. Knowing God began with kind intentions towards us gives us confidence that He is committed to our good and not to our harm. How could a loving Creator create something in His image and end up not liking what He made? That type of thought process denies the grace-based salvation narrative we see in the Scriptures. Genesis 1:28 goes on to tell us that the Lord God blessed humanity after they were made in His image and likeness.

Let's examine the Hebrew word for "blessing," so that we understand what was in God's heart for people when we hear "God blessed them." Barak is the Hebrew word for bless in the Scriptures. It means to bless, praise or have divine favor spoken over you. This is an amazing concept to understand that God blessed, praised, and imputed humanity with divine favor. Even an elementary revelation of this truth can open deep thoughts of His love for us and encourage us to believe that God likes us.

Many people believe divine pleasure comes into our lives by religious performances and keeping promises we make to God. However, when we look at this first revelation of God's heart for those made in His image and likeness, we see He liked what He made and spoke affirmation and acceptance over humanity. God founded humanity in grace, and He continues to relate to us in grace today.

After the Lord blessed them, He gave them a mandate to be fruitful. This Hebrew word is parah, and it means to be fruitful, to branch off, and to cause to bear fruit. It is a verb which carries the idea that as we co-labor with God in fulfilling His spoken destiny over us, we would experience prosperity and fullness in our lives. When we think of bearing fruit, we should think in terms of experiencing the goodness of God in whatever we put our hands to. The clear context of the word here is the expansion of the human family. Along with family come the many blessings of destiny, marriage, provision, children, and the happiness of experiencing and seeing the fruit of love in our lives.

The next movement we see in Genesis 1:28 is God gave humanity the grace to multiply. The Hebrew word for multiply is rabah (another verb), which means to become great, numerous, to do much, or to grow into greatness. When we look at the concepts of both these words joined together – "fruitful and multiply" - we can see that the Lord extended the grace for people to accomplish His desire for them as they moved in agreement with His word. The Lord never intended for people to live in a state that was devoid of His grace and goodness.

The last movement in Genesis 1:28 is the mandate to subdue and rule over creation. We will look at these two Hebrew words and explore their definitions, unpacking the truth held in the concepts related to their understandings. The Hebrew word for "subdue" is kabash, and means to subject, subdue, or force. The Hebrew word for rule is radah and means to have dominion or to tread down. These two verbs have very strong meanings. So, what type of "subduing and ruling" did God have in mind?

When we think about subduing and ruling creation, we are thinking in terms of creation care and the reformation of the earth to reflect God. It is basically this: Those made in God's image and likeness are given the grace and authority to reform the earth, along with all creation contained in the earth, to re-image it into looking like God's character and nature. This is a prophetic picture of the mission of the Church of Jesus Christ. Our mission is not just to spread salvation knowledge, but to disciple nations and reform systems to operate in ways that reflect God's heart. Our knowledge of God will determine that outcome. If we believe God is angry, then we will re-image God as a God who is angry with humanity and is looking for an opportunity to bring His wrath. However, having a grace-filled and love-motivated view of God will re-image Him as One who is ready to partner with humanity to experience His best for them. As members of the global Body of Christ, we can deeply affect the condition of this planet. A healed perspective of what God is like will determine the result.

To summarize, we can see God is kind and good. He likes people! He has extended to them grace and authority to accomplish their mission as humanity, to re-image God in the world in order to reflect His heart.

Of course, all these things were spoken over humanity before the Fall. But understanding God's original intent is the key to understanding God's purpose of forgiveness and redemption in Jesus Christ, His Son. Jesus, being the Second Adam, brought about the process of restoring God's original intent. Now, let's look at the process God used to restore original intent to us.

When we say, "original intent," what does it mean? The definition of original intent in its simplest understanding is God relating to each one of us in love, pleasure, goodness, mercy and the restoration of the relationship God had with Adam and Eve, the representatives of mankind before the Fall in Eden. The Scriptures teach us that God has a salvation narrative which consists of a series of interactions with Himself and people. The ultimate crescendo is the death, resurrection, and ascension of Jesus Christ, the New Covenant firmly established, and finally the second coming of Jesus Christ unto eternity. If we looked at the Scriptures with this in view, we would see the whole of human history as an exciting epoch of God fathering humanity to greatness, and ultimately the restoration of His original intent.

We have learned that God founded the creation of humanity in a relationship of love, grace, and the empowerment to fulfill a destiny: to re-image God on the earth as humanity multiplied and subdued it. This is called the Edenic Covenant. The Lord related to humanity in a completely grace-based covenant of friendship and goodwill. Even after the

Fall with Adam and Eve's exile from Eden, there were still covenant benefits that continued to touch humanity. Regarding the Fall, we see several movements and declarations of God that are worth mentioning before we move on.

It is important to note the Lord did not "child-proof" Eden. Satan, represented as the serpent, had access to God's children in Eden just as he had influence to lead an angelic rebellion against God in heaven and turn angelic hearts away from God. With this in mind, we are pointed to two truths which communicate to us that God is love (1 John 4:8).

The first truth is that God created Adam and Eve with the free-will capacity to choose to love God or to choose a lie about God. When we look at the Scriptural concept of love, we see that love is a free-will choice of an individual to either choose to love or to receive love. In the context of Eden, the choice presented to them was the choice to love God, trusting Him for their care to carry out their mandate in the grace of God's favor and blessing. The other side of that choice was to believe a lie about

God, choosing not to love or trust Him, and to doubt the intentions of His heart toward them. Unfortunately, they choose to believe the lie about God. If we look at the world today, we can see humanity is still choosing the lie, therefore, living in an inferior reality of life. Love is not love unless one has the choice to choose it.

The second truth is that God honors free-will. God gave value to humanity by giving us the power of self-will or choice. Our free-will choice mimics the sovereignty of God as ones made in His image. What is amazing is that the Lord is engaged in the process of working out His salvation narrative through the free-will choices of individuals that are responding to His love. The scale of this theological thought is so vast it is almost beyond comprehension! But for the sake of simplicity, let's just say that God loves people so much that He gave them the authority to choose love and God honors their choices.

In response to Adam and Eve's choice to not live in a reality of love and trust in God in Genesis 3, God cursed two things: The Serpent and the ground. If blessing is divine favor, then cursing is the absence of divine favor. It is important to note that the serpent/Satan is in a state of being that is devoid of the favor of God. This should encourage us because our enemy has no grace to triumph in his cause for sin, death and the separation of people from God. His gain in Eden is temporary and shrinking as the gospel of Jesus Christ is extended throughout the earth in the hearts and minds of people.

The second object of the curse is the ground - or for a more comprehensive thought - the whole natural realm. This concept is unpacked for us in detail in Romans 8:18-22. The realm in which we live and breathe is subject to corruption, evil influence and death. These are the fruits of the Fall in Eden.

There was a Fall in Eden, but there also was a promise. In Genesis 3:15, the Lord promised there would be a Deliver who would completely defeat the serpent and crush his head. The imagery in Genesis 3:15 prophesies a decisive and devastating victory over the serpent which Jesus Christ accomplished on the cross. The whole story of Scripture is the unfolding of the promise of restored humanity and a restored Eden.

To summarize, we have learned that God is good, full of grace, and gave humanity a mandate to co-rule with Him as they heavenized earth. After the Fall, the Lord re-empowered His grace with a promise which was fulfilled in Jesus Christ. Now that the promise of the Messiah has been fulfilled in Jesus and people are being reconciled to the Father through Christ, the invitation to heavenize earth is lived out as Christians lead Spirit-led lives, impacting their world around them.

CONNECT GROUP QUESTIONS

1 – Genesis presents God's nature and character as wholly benevolent and good from the beginning. How is the reputation of God perceived in our society? In what ways can Christians better communicate God's original intent for people?

2 – Genesis 3 introduces us to the concept of personalized evil and spiritual warfare at a macro-level. What was the main lie about God that is the root from

which temptation follows?

3 – The promise of Messiah in Genesis 3:15 points to the defeat of the serpent and the mandate for humanity to co-labor with God is re-established. In what ways can Christians co-labor with God to bring the knowledge of Him and the benefits of His kingdom to our society?

Chapter Two

HIS STORY, HIS PROMISES

When we look at Scripture, we should see it as the process of God unveiling the promise that the He gave humanity in Genesis 3:15. In the first chapter of this book, we learned that God is good, fatherly to all He made, restorative and committed to fulfilling His promise to humanity through a Deliverer who would come and defeat the serpent. The entire Bible tells the narrative of the unfolding process of how God works to restore the Eden which was lost to sin. The Lord uses the process of covenants to promise, prophesy and reveal the Deliverer, Jesus Christ. These covenants move the salvation narrative closer to fulfillment in Christ, communicating information about God's nature and character as they progress towards Messiah.

The first covenant God makes with humanity in Eden was to be fruitful, multiply, fill the earth and rule the created order. In terms of revealing God's goodness, we see that first covenant God makes with humanity is a covenant of grace in the context of real relationship. To be fruitful, multiply and manage His creation requires favor and the active abundance God gives in His kindness towards people. God is generous and full of grace. This is how His story begins.

The next covenant God makes with humanity is after the Flood. The Scriptures say the Lord God was grieved with the level of sin that was being manifested in people and He decided to judge sin in humanity by flooding the earth. In the middle of the thought in which God was regretting He had made mankind, the Bible says, "but Noah found favor in the eyes of the Lord." This shows us that Noah is a type of Messiah who delivered the whole human race from the judgment of sin by being an obedient son, building the ark, thus saving humanity. We see one man saving humanity; a proto-gospel. When Noah emerged from the ark, he worshipped the Lord in sacrifice and the Lord reaffirms the grace-based mandate to be fruitful, multiply and fill the earth. We can believe the Lord desires many sons and daughters to be in relationship with Him. We also see the Genesis 3:15 promise move closer to fulfillment in Christ.

To summarize, we see Noah - whose name means comfort - reveals to us an appeal to the promise that God made to humanity that Noah might deliver humanity from the curse on the earth. We see God finding favor in one man, who would deliver the whole human race from judgment. Lastly, we see God reaffirming His benevolent goodness by giving humanity the grace to prosper. We see a Father committed to sons and daughters, and a Father who is committed to the process of delivering them.

As we travel through the salvation narrative, we find the third covenant as we see God calling Abram out and inviting him to go on a journey with Him. We see the Lord interacting with Abram as God befriends and fathers Abram to the point of a promise where he becomes Abraham. God's promise to Abraham was that through his seed, all the nations and people groups of the earth would be blessed, and Abraham would have offspring as numerous as the grains of the sand. Galatians 3 teaches us the promised seed was Jesus Christ. We see the salvation narrative move forward and the gospel of Jesus Christ coming into view. The faith of Abraham became the faith of those who would place their hope in his Seed, Jesus Christ, and through faith in Christ many sons and daughters would become not only His children but become the children of Abraham, too. God fulfilled His promise to Abraham as the gospel reaps a harvest in the nations of the world. Abraham did not work for God's approval or promise, Abraham believed God's promise and his faith became the breakthrough for the people of faith. God moved in His covenant with Abraham based on grace through faith, and through God's relationship with Abraham we see the gospel prophesied in advance. It is revealed to us for the third time that grace is God's primary approach to humanity.

As the salvation narrative progresses, more information about God's nature and character is being revealed and more information about the promised Messiah is coming to the front and center.

The fourth covenant God uses to reveal, and prophesy Christ is His covenant with Moses and the Israelites. The Lord begins to narrow the salvation narrative by bringing the promised Seed, Christ, into view as He works through Israel. Israel is the womb by which Messiah would be revealed to the world, and the people through which God would reveal Himself as He relates to them as their husband or covenant partner. They would be His people; He would be their God. In Exodus 19, the Lord offers the Israelites a grace-based relationship with Himself, that they would be a kingdom of priests and a holy nation who would be a people that would reveal God to the nations. As we know, the Lord comes in a consuming fire to Mt. Sinai and the people choose fear over relationship and reject the grace-based relationship God is offering to them. The Lord honors their hearts and gives them the Law through Moses. Now the Law becomes the standard by which God relates to His people, and the perfect Law governs imperfect people.

Through the Law, God reveals His holiness and humanity learns that imperfection can never fulfill a perfect Law.

In Galatians 3, it says the Law becomes a tutor to lead us to Christ. The Law also reveals Christ to be a perfect Law-Keeper. If all humanity are law breakers, then Messiah must be a perfect Law-Keeper. Jesus says in Matthew that He did not come to abolish the Law, but to fulfill the Law. If Jesus fulfills the Law, then He is a perfect, sinless Son of God. The salvation narrative moves forward in the frustration of the Law because the works of the Law reveal our complete dependence on the Deliverer whom God promised in Genesis 3:15. We should think of the Mosaic Law in these terms: the fourth covenant was offered as a grace-based covenant in which God's people would be a kingdom of priests, but because of their fear and rejection at Sinai, God gave them the Law which would become God's standard to reveal sin. In addition to this, Jesus would be revealed as the Second Adam, the only Son to completely obey God. Jesus would represent the whole mass of humanity like Adam represented the whole mass of humanity. The first Adam failed. The Second Adam prevailed. The covenant at Sinai - the Old Covenant - stands out in the salvation narrative because one relates to God through the Law, contrasted to the three other covenants that God made which were based upon the goodness and grace of God.

The fifth covenant God made with David pushes the salvation narrative forward and prophesies the Messiah would be an authoritative King who would rule an everlasting kingdom. David's gratitude towards the Lord had overflowed to the point where David put it into his heart to build the Lord a house. Of course, the Lord fills all creation, but David desired a permanent place of presence and intimate meeting where God would be worshipped, praised and sought after. The Lord responds with kindness towards David's request by granting it through Solomon, but the Lord responds to David himself with a promise. David would have a Son who would rule on his throne forever in an everlasting dominion over the nations of the earth. The Lord gives David a grace-based promise where David did not have to perform for the promise, but only receive it.

As we look at the history of Israel through the era of the kings, we see a people struggling with God, disobeying His commands in the Law, and eventually being exiled into Babylon. Through the era of the kings, the Lord would raise up prophets who would prophesy according to God's heart and invite the people back to Himself over and over through their prophecies. These prophecies brought the Messiah who would come into view, and with these prophecies the promise of a New Covenant. In Jeremiah 31:13, Jeremiah prophesies the Lord would put His Law into the hearts of His people, and they would relate to Him in grace through faith and not Law. Through the era of the kings and prophets, the wonderful and amazing fore-telling of Jesus being born in Bethlehem; Jesus atoning for sin; Jesus being raised from the dead; and His Messianic victory over the powers of darkness come to pass in striking detail of living color in the Man, Christ Jesus.

Jesus Christ fulfills all the types and shadows of the salvation narrative that God uses to weave His glory story of being faithful to bring about what He had promised in Genesis 3:15. Jesus cut the New Covenant, the sixth and final covenant, which was prophesied on the cross and now Jesus, being raised from the dead and ascended to heaven, sits on David's throne ruling and reigning at the right hand of the Father. Now God, through faith in Jesus Christ, receives sons and daughters and begins to bring to a crescendo the salvation narrative at the second coming of His Son. We should now see the purpose of the Old Covenant scripture was to tell the story of how God makes good on His promises.

In the next chapter we will explore the scope of the atonement in the New Covenant, and how this changes everything in terms of our relationship with God and our relationship to the world around us.

CONNECT GROUP QUESTIONS
1 – Have you considered the Scriptures to be a unified and progressive narrative of how God makes good on His promise of a Messiah who would decisively destroy Satan in Genesis 3:15?

2 – Does seeing the salvation narrative in a series of progressive covenants empower you to think more confidently about God and about our identity in Him?

3 – Even though this chapter is a very simple overview of how God moved in history to reveal Messiah, what are some deeper thoughts that you might be thinking about the Lord and how would these deeper thoughts encourage you in your faith?

Chapter Three

JESUS HEALS THE WHOLE PERSON

Isaiah 53 is one of the most beautiful and deep prophesies of the suffering of Jesus and His work of atonement in all the Bible. We also have the wonderful prophesies of the glory of His kingdom and triumph that would follow in Isaiah 54. Considering the suffering and the promised glory of Jesus, there are some specifics regarding the dimensions of the atonement in Jesus' death on the cross that have tremendous implications when we join them to our faith. Isaiah 53:4-6 outlines a snapshot of the scope of the benefits extended to humanity in living color that causes us to realize that Jesus' atonement was much more than a promise of heaven after life on earth. Our English translations struggle to reveal the fullness of the Hebrew texts in terms of what is possible regarding the atonement of Jesus Christ. In addition to this, a literal rendering of the Hebrew words places a demand on the Christian to believe deeper and wider than we may have previously believed possible in the cross.

Isaiah 53:4-6 – "Surely, he took up our pain and bore our suffering, yet we considered him punished by God, stricken by him, and afflicted. But he was pierced for our transgressions, he was crushed for our iniquities; the punishment that brought us peace was on him, and by his wounds we are healed. We all, like sheep, have gone astray, each of us has turned to our own way; and the LORD has laid on him the iniquity of us all." – NIV

Isaiah 53:4 declares "surely he took up our pain." In some translations, "pain" is translated "griefs." The Hebrew word is *khol·ē'* which means, quite literally, *sickness or disease.* This is wonderful news because the text expressly speaks to us that Jesus "took up" our physical pain and disease in His body on the cross. This implies healing and freedom from pain in our physical bodies is a New Covenant benefit and a right for every believer. In fact, Matthew 8:17 says, "This was to fulfill what was spoken through the prophet Isaiah: "He took up our infirmities and bore our diseases." Matthew directly applies this verse to Jesus in the context

of healing and deliverance. Notice
Matthew says "fulfill" in verse 17 implying
that, in Jesus, the fullness of the healing
promise is revealed.

The next amazing Hebrew word in
Isaiah 53:4 is *mak·ōve'* for which our translators use the English word "suffering" or
"sorrows." The Hebrew word *mak·ōve'*
literally means *physical pain and mental
pain*. This adds another layer of physical
healing, but also opens the possibility for
healing our mental pain, brokenness and
trauma that life can bring. There emerges
an inner-healing dimension which promises our traumas, insecurities, addictions,
mental illness and emotional pain can
be healed in Christ. We should see Jesus,
the Man of Suffering, empathizing and
understanding the brokenness of the
human experience in this fallen world. The
Gospels present Jesus as the God/Man
who forgives sin, extends mercy, breaks
demonic strongholds, brings justice
to what is wrong, demonstrates the love
of the Father, teaches us the Father's
heart, and empowers us to live these
realities in Him. Isaiah 53:4 prophesies to
us that Jesus Christ's ministry and His work
of atonement releases healing grace

in every area of our lives that need His touch.

Isaiah 53:4 presents the thought that people had considered Christ stricken and afflicted by God or punished by God. When we look at the cross of Christ, we can either see a man suffering or see a beautiful act of obedience to the Father with love for humanity in His suffering. How we view the atonement is the key to experiencing the promises of healing, physical and mental, or deliverance from strongholds in our life. Either we see the promise and marry that promise to faith, or we see the suffering with no benefit and miss the glory of the atonement. The compass of our heart determines the manifestation of the atonement.

In Isaiah 53:5, deep dimensions of forgiveness of sin are revealed. Verse five says, "But he was pierced for our transgressions, he was crushed for our iniquities." The two Hebrew words used for "transgressions" and "iniquities" reveal the holistic forgiveness that Christ brings to our personal sins we have committed against God and people. The nail wounds of Christ and His pierced side satisfied the demand of justice from the Father for the offense of sin in humanity. The Hebrew word for "transgressions" is *peh' ·shah*, which means *rebellion in every expression of rebellion in humanity*: Rebellion against God, rebellion against our fellow people, and rebellion against nations. This describes our willful sins committed because of our selfish and unloving nature apart from Christ. Forgiveness for all the ways we have missed the mark and chose wrongdoing is paid for and given in the atonement.

The next word to key in on is the Hebrew word for "iniquities" which is *ä ·vōn'*. The definition of this Hebrew word is *depravity, guilt, and iniquity*. We could say that *ä ·vōn'* stands for the resident wrongdoing and turmoil that resides in all of us from the Fall. The New Testament word that corresponds to *ä ·vōn'* would be *the flesh* or *sarx* in the Greek. We are all aware that none of us are perfect and we are weak in many ways. We have all tasted the bitter defeat of losing the battle between right and wrong in our lives. The good news is that the cross atones for every way which sin is manifested in people.

Isaiah 53:5 concludes with the most glorious words in Scripture, "the punishment that brought us peace was on him, and by his wounds we are healed." The cross of Christ brings us peace and the wounding of Christ extends to us healing in every dimension of the human experience. The Hebrew word for "peace" is *shä·lōm'* which is *a holistic peace in every expression that peace can be experienced. Shä·lōm'* is peace with God; peace within; peace with those in our proximity; and peace in our nation to the point of ceasing from war. Jesus is truly revealed as the Prince of Peace when His people increase in a nation and extend that peace to others. All peace flows from peace with God. If we are at peace with God, that means there is no offense between us and Him. We can have confidence that we are good with Him and are living in the shadow of His grace and love when we receive the Father's offer of forgiveness by faith in the sacrifice of Jesus Christ. Shame no longer has a place in the hearts of those who know these truths.

Isaiah 53:6 concludes the atonement with a reinforcement of the purpose of the sufferings of Christ as verse six declares, "We all, like sheep, have gone astray, each of us has turned to our own way; and the LORD has laid on him the iniquity of us all." Very plainly we, like sheep, have strayed. The very imagery of sheep in this text shapes our thoughts to realize that sheep need to be led, fed, cared for and protected by a Shepherd who made every provision for the healing and well-being of His sheep. No human is divorced from the effects of sin in their lives and grace flows from Christ on the cross. Jesus paid for every sin committed in humanity from the Fall to the end of the age. What amazing grace is shown to us in the cross!

Grace does not end there because Christians have been given the gift of the Holy Spirit and we have been given a new nature. The result of this is that we are no longer subject to the flesh, the guilt and the sin that separates us from God. The Lord has extended everything we need for life and godliness in this lifetime. While we are not perfect, we are being perfected as we are conformed to image of Christ in every season of our walk in Him. This reveals that God is engaged and intimately involved in the process of maturing sons and daughters to His glory as a patient Father and loving God who gently guides, teaches and encourages us over the course of a life path. Christianity lives in the everyday experience of the life of the believer. The atoning grace of God brings into view the beauty of the life of the Christian.

CONNECT GROUP QUESTIONS

1 – Are there any areas of your life where the grace, mercy, freedom from guilt, regret and forgiveness of God need to be experienced?

2 – Is there an area of your life where you need to be healed in your body or in your soul? What role does faith play as you experience healing, or wait for God's healing to be revealed in your life?

3 – In what ways have you experienced peace in Christ? How can you personally give the peace of Christ away to the people in your life? Do you need to forgive anyone so that you may experience peace in a greater level?

Chapter Four

GIFTS OF THE HOLY SPIRIT

1 Corinthians 12:7-11 – "Now to each one the manifestation of the Spirit is given for the common good. To one there is given through the Spirit a message of wisdom, to another a message of knowledge by means of the same Spirit, to another faith by the same Spirit, to another gifts of healing by that one Spirit, to another miraculous powers, to another prophecy, to another distinguishing between spirits, to another speaking in different kinds of tongues, and to still another the interpretation of tongues. All these are the work of one and the same Spirit, and he distributes them to each one, just as he determines." – NIV

It is has become continually more acceptable in the last 60 years for American Christians to believe in the continuance of the supernatural gifts of the Holy Spirit. This is great because an Apostolic (Early Christian) expression of Christianity included signs and wonders that authenticate the existence of the Kingdom of God and the messengers who are preaching its gospel. In many ways, one could look at the overview of Christian history and see God fathering His Church through the centuries, restoring Apostolic expression and truth. In the first 400 years of the Church, we were wrestling with truth about the Person of Christ, the Trinity and writing confessions of faith that bound us in the unity of faith. These confessions of faith still stand today. The next era was one of evangelizing the known world and establishing Christianity on multiple continents. The Middle Ages, after the fall of the Roman Empire, brought the Dark Ages with the loss of literacy and technology. This era was one that witnessed the Church splitting from West to East and the expression of Christianity changed drastically. In this, the Reformation emerged to pioneer the return of Biblical truth regarding salvation, Christian customs and the wonderful movement of Bible literacy in the common people. Next, we had the great revivals of Wesley, Finney, and others who set the stage for the Azusa Street revival; the Charismatic Movements of the mid 1900's; and finally, the emergence of the New Apostolic Reformation. In this very brief macroview of Church History, we can see God's guiding presence in His people leading them back to an expression of the Church that is beginning to look again like the Early Church era. This is great news because when the Church reflects the Apostolic Era, wide and rapid evangelistic harvest is accelerated.

So much has been written about the gifts of the Holy Spirit that this chapter will not do this topic justice. However, the point of this chapter is to gain the understanding that the gifts of the Spirit are purposeful and necessary if Christians are to accomplish the Great Commission in Matthew 28. The expression of the sign gifts of the Holy Spirit are indicators of the health of our local churches and their expression of power is a measurable, seen metric by which we can gauge how God is really among us. In this chapter, we look at the definitions of the sign gifts of the Holy Spirit, how they are expressed and why we should practice them. Finally, we will look at modern evangelical objections to supernatural power in the

Church and answer their objections.

The best place to start is 1 Corinthians 12 where the Apostle Paul begins to correct and explain the gifts of the Holy Spirit to the Church in Corinth. He starts in verse one, pointing their attention to the truth that Christians should not be uninformed about the gifts. The word in the Greek is agneo, where we get our English word ignorant. Paul is telling Christians very plainly that we should understand the gifts of the Holy Spirit. We should receive his teaching and correction about which gifts are more useful and how to express them in a local body of believers.

In 1 Corinthians 12:7, Paul writes the purpose of the expression of the gifts of the Holy Spirit is for the "common good." This is the beautiful Greek word *symphero*. This Greek word indicates that any time the gifts of the Holy Spirit are practiced in the local church, common good is released into the church. The gifts should bring out the goodness of God and benefit us in their use. If we look at the list of these gifts, we can see how wonderful the gift of healing is because we are touched in a personal way by God and our testimony raises the faith of our brothers and sisters who hear about the goodness of God in our lives. A powerful prophetic promise keeps us focused on our journey in Christ and keeps us dependent on Him and encouraged as we pursue our callings and destinies together. In in many other ways, the goodness of God is communicated through the gifts of the Spirit operating through Christians.

In 1 Corinthians 12:8, we are introduced to the list of the supernatural gifts of the Holy Spirit which should be operating in the local church. Verse 8 starts with the first two gifts and moves on from there. We should think the supernatural would be normal for the Christian experience and expression of our faith. God is naturally supernatural, and with God in us as the Person of the Holy Spirit, we should never believe supernatural expressions in God's people are rare or not possible.

Verse 8 is also clear that the gifts of the Holy Spirit are given to His people as a revelation of His grace. The first two gifts of the Holy Spirit mentioned are the "message of wisdom" and a "message of knowledge or word of knowledge." A message of wisdom is the ability to know divine things; to form and to work God's will; and the act of interpreting dreams, visions or numbers. It is basically to know what God thinks or feels about a matter. This is a very powerful gift because if a Christian can know what God wants to do about something, then the strategies of success and influence are available to the church. This gift makes supernatural knowledge relevant and practical in its application.

The next gift mentioned in verse 8 is the "message of knowledge or word of knowledge." This gift is usually expressed in the ability to know something by supernatural knowledge from the Holy Spirit. Jesus modeled this gift in Mark 2:7 when He perceived in His spirit that the scribes were questioning within themselves that only God forgives sin. The word of knowledge gift can be any piece of supernatural knowledge, as in someone in need of a specific healing, the name of a person who the Lord wants to minister to, personal addresses, phone numbers, and other pieces of information given to reveal God's love, mercy and healing power to people.

As we continue to move through 1 Corinthians 12:7-11, verse 9 lists two more gifts of the Holy Spirit: the "gift of faith" and "gifts of healing." The gift of faith is the supernatural ability to trust what God says is true. The Greek word is *pistis* which means a strong conviction of belief in something. This is an immovable posture of the soul that will not relent to unbelief and simply trusts God's written word, prophetic word or other supernatural revelation as it applies to a current circumstance. People with the gift of faith can be tremendous encouragers in the middle of a struggle. This gift moves way beyond the general grace of faith which every Christian possesses for salvation and trusting God for Christian living. It is the type of faith that is supernaturally empowered by the Holy Spirit.

The next gift we see in verse 9 is "gifts of healing." Our translators used "gifts," plural, because the Greek word for healing, *iama*, is a holistic word for healing and any method in which healing may be manifested. Healing could come in the form of supernatural declarations and prayers of healing. Inner healing could come by the Holy Spirit through an anointed person, or any mode of healing facilitated by supernatural interaction with the Holy Spirit and the person ministering the healing. This leaves the door wide open in terms of how healing would be manifested through God's sons and daughters. It is a very encouraging thought that the Lord would partner with His children to minister healing to another with the Person of the Holy Spirit guiding the healing process. The glory of supernatural healing is that the love, kindness and mercy of God is revealed in ways that cannot be denied.

I Corinthians 12:10 lists five gifts of the Holy Spirit that are given to the Church. Each of these gifts are tremendously powerful and useful for the Church. The first gift mentioned in verse 10 is "miracles," or *energēma dynamis* in the Greek. The definitions of these Greek words are loose in this context and we could say that miracles would be any possibility where supernatural power is manifested to glorify God. The examples we see in Scripture would be the multiplication of bread, walking on water, calming a storm, resurrection of the dead, an axe head floating, etc. The definition of these Greek words should encourage us to expect God would do great and amazing things through the hands of His people who walk in this gift. The expectation of the manifestation of this gift should be wide and deep, not constricted by the bounds of this universe. The possibilities are endless.

The next gift in the list is "prophecy." There has been more written about this gift in the modern Church era than any other gift of the Holy Spirit. It certainly is the gift that the Apostle Paul champions in 1 Corinthians as the most important because the gift of prophecy encourages and edifies the Church. Our short description of this gift is not exhaustive but will point our attention to the truths in the Scripture and will give us a good working definition of the gift. The word in Greek is *prophēteia*, which carries a multi-dimensional definition. The gift of prophecy can be expressed as a discourse that is led by the Holy Spirit to declare the purposes of God. It can be a rebuke that is given under the leading of the

Holy Spirit. Prophecy can manifest in words that bring comfort to the hurting and discouraged. Prophecy can be the fore-telling of coming events, or the revelation of hidden things not known to the one prophesying. We can see just by the expanded definition that the possibilities of how the gift of prophecy is expressed and applied can be diverse. We see expressions of this gift all through the book of Acts in the lives of Stephen, Phillip's four daughters, and Agabus. Much more could be written about prophecy, but the point is to consider that this gift is useful, good and purposeful for God's people - the Church.

The next gift is "discerning of spirits," or in the Greek, *diakrisis pneuma*. This gift is perhaps the most abused and misunderstood gift in the modern church era. There are many evangelicals who have so called "discernment" ministries that exist to criticize charismatic and Pentecostal brothers and sisters. Their expression of the gift is not by the Holy Spirit and does not employ any attempt of partnering with the Holy Spirit. I would characterize these ministries as "doctrinal purity tests" that brand any expression of

Christianity that they do not like as wrong and dangerous.

The Greek words, *diakrisis pneuma*, simply mean to judge spirits. For one to judge spirits, one needs to supernaturally "see" or discern the spirits that are operating. This would be the supernatural ability by the Holy Spirit to know the spiritual climate of a location, region or city, see a spirit (angel or demon), understand the assignment of these spirits and know what to do about them. We can see that radio programs, podcasts and blogs condemning charismatic Christianity fall short of the biblical definition of the words. This gift is necessary especially in the context of spiritual warfare, intercession and prayer because to understand the spiritual realm is to know the strategy of prayer for breakthrough. This is a gift that needs to be better understood and utilized so that the Church will have greater success in evangelism and cultural authority.

The next gift in the list is the gift of "tongues." This gift used to be controversial, but most of the controversy has subsided among believers because of the common use and great benefits that this gift has given the Church in the modern era. The Greek word for tongues is *glōssa*, which means unknown or known languages. This is the supernatural ability to speak in languages that are unknown to the speaker or known only by the Holy Spirit. Scripture teaches us two things about the expression of this gift. The first is that it reveals and glorifies God, as in Acts 2 at the Pentecostal outpouring of the Holy Spirit. The second thing that is mentioned about this gift is in 1 Corinthians 14:4 where Paul writes the gift of tongues edifies the believer. The word for edify in the Greek is oikodomeo, which means to build or erect a house. This means we are supernaturally built up in the inner-person in ways that support our faith in Christ. The two gifts that are manifested when people are filled with the Holy Spirit in the book of Acts are tongues and prophecy. This is a great gift that should be sought and practiced because of its supernatural ability to build up the believer.

The last gift of the Holy Spirit mentioned is the gift of "interpretation of tongues." The Greek word for interpretation is *hermeneia*, which means interpretation or revealing what is obscured by words. This is simply the supernatural understanding and interpretation of tongues. This is very useful in an assembly where someone speaks in a tongue so that everyone present may be encouraged and be given the opportunity to understand the message. It is apparent why Paul would prefer the Corinthians to prophesy because prophecy should be the native language of a believer. We should always desire an interpretation in corporate settings whenever possible, for the encouragement and edification of the church body. We will not discuss any further about this gift as tongues and interpretation of tongues is becoming more common in the Body of Christ, and many Christians have witnessed them in use.

Paul goes on to write in 1 Corinthians 12:11 that all these gifts operate by the Holy Spirit and they are given "as He wills." This is important because it gives the proper context on why God would give supernatural gifts of the Holy Spirit to His children. The gifts are for building up His Church, making us inter-dependent with one another, while also having us dependent upon the Holy Spirit. Perhaps in the Western Church, we have lost the exhilarating experience of witnessing the use of the gifts, seeing God work through each other in ways that bring Him glory and fame.

Paul inserts the great love passage of 1 Corinthians 13:1-13 in the context of spiritual gifts and their expression. This teaches us that the purpose of spiritual power is the expression of love, encouragement, comforting and strengthening of His people. What a beautiful concept, that we would love using the gifts of the Holy Spirit in powerful and dramatic ways that would cause us to be inter-dependent and reliant on God all at the same time. Lastly, there is no place in the New Testament Scriptures where it expressly says the gifts of the Holy Spirit have ceased. A certain passage where critics point to is 1 Corinthians 13:8-9. A quick review of the Greek text teaches us that the "completion" or "finishing" comes at the end of this age in the return of Jesus Christ. As long as there is a Church on the earth in this age, we will need the gifts to accomplish the purposes of God: to encourage, heal, strengthen, and comfort one another.

CONNECT GROUP QUESTIONS

1 – After reading this chapter, what are the gifts of the Holy Spirit that you personally believe you are walking in? In what ways has the Holy Spirit moved through you to bring encouragement, comfort and strength to the people around you?

2 – How can the Church express the gifts of the Spirit in a way that would make them more accessible to every person in the congregation? How can the expression of supernatural power enhance evangelism?

3 – Are there any gifts of the Holy Spirit that you would desire from the list in 1 Corinthians 12:7-11 that you do not already have? Take time to pray for one another and ask the Holy Spirit to impart these gifts to one another.

Chapter Five

APOSTLES AND PROPHETS

Ephesians 4:11-13 - "So Christ himself gave the apostles, the prophets, the evangelists, the pastors and teachers, to equip his people for works of service, so that the body of Christ may be built up until we all reach unity in the faith and in the knowledge of the Son of God and become mature, attaining to the whole measure of the fullness of Christ." - NIV

One of the defining marks of the Apostolic Reformation movement is the belief that God is restoring the governmental offices of Apostle and Prophet for the leading and administration of the Church in the modern era. The first person to discern this and point it out is the late Dr. C. Peter Wagner in his seminal book Apostles and Prophets. Dr. Wagner spent much of his time defining and developing the Apostolic Reformation Movement because he believed from his scholarly research that God was doing something significant and impactful in the Church of the modern era. Dr. Wagner pointed out that Church history from the post-Apostolic era, to the Reformation, to the Azusa Street Revivals, to the Third Wave Movement, God was moving through history to restore the expression of Apostolic Christianity so that the Church would mature in its mission and calling to convert the world to Christ. Much has been said and much has been written about this subject, and this chapter does not have space to give an exhaustive treatment of the topic. However, this chapter will help us understand why we should believe Apostles and Prophets would be leading God's Church and help dispel the controversy that some evangelical Christians have concerning the 5-Fold Ministry of governing God's Church.

The first place we should start is to understand the biblical basis for believing that Apostles and Prophets are necessary for the governing and administration of the Church. In the previous chapter, we learned about the gifts of the Holy Spirit and made the case for the for the continuance of the gifts of the Holy Spirit for the edification, strengthening, comfort and encouraging of the Church. We also learned that the gifts of the Spirit created inter-dependence in God's people and help to make us dependent upon the Holy Spirit for the graces with which we serve one another. Lastly, we learned there is not an express command or exhortation in Scripture for the ceasing of the gifts of the Holy Spirit. If there is not cessation of the gifts of the Holy Spirit, then the offices God has ordained to govern the Spirit-filled Church have not ceased either. This is the reason why the Church should expect the 5-Fold offices of Church government to continue throughout the Church age.

Ephesians 4:11 says that "Christ himself gave the apostles, prophets, evangelists, pastors and teachers" to equip, reach unity, and mature to the point of fullness in the Church. This verse teaches us that these gifted people were given to the Church for the process of healing, maturing, equipping and releasing the people of the Church into the work of the ministry. The work of the ministry and the need to heal and mature Christians has not changed in almost 2000 years of history. Most Christians are comfortable with the titles of evangelist, pastor and teacher but are resistant to the titles of apostle and prophet. Most of the objection comes from the belief that there were only 12 apostles whom Jesus called. But if we look at the Scriptures, we can see Jesus called more than 12 apostles and there were prophets who ministered in the Church as well. Let's look at some Scriptures that support our position:

Jesus called the original 12 apostles
Matthew 10:1-4 - "Jesus called his twelve disciples to him and gave them authority to drive out impure spirits and to heal every disease and sickness. These are the names of the twelve apostles: first, Simon (who is called Peter) and his brother Andrew; James son of Zebedee, and his brother John; Philip and Bartholomew; Thomas and Matthew the tax collector; James son of Alphaeus, and Thaddaeus; Simon the Zealot and Judas Iscariot, who betrayed him."

Judas was replaced by Matthias
Acts 1:26 - "Then they cast lots, and the lot fell to Matthias; so he was added to the eleven apostles."

Paul was called an Apostle
1 Corinthians 15:9 - "For I am the least of the apostles and do not even deserve to be called an apostle, because I persecuted the church of God."

James, Jesus half-brother, was also recognized as an apostle
1 Corinthians 15:7 - "Then he appeared to James, then to all the apostles; Galatians 1:19 - I saw none of the other apostles — only James, the Lord's brother."

Two more apostles in Rome: Andronicus and Junia (a female apostle)
Romans 16:7 - "Greet Andronicus and Junia, my fellow Jews who have been in prison with me. They are outstanding among the apostles, and they were in Christ before I was."

From this brief survey of Scripture, we learn the following things: Jesus called 12 original apostles, but after His death and resurrection, the apostolic office was widened to others who were not part of the original 12 for the expansion and governing of the Church. In Acts 15, we see James - not part of the original 12 - calling an apostolic council to determine what Gentile believers needed to do to be added to Israel. James sent them a letter that they only needed to believe in Jesus Christ for saving faith, they were not to commit sexual immorality, and they were not to consume blood. In this instance, we see James having more authority over Peter and Paul because they submitted to James' authority as the leader of the mother Church in Jerusalem. Would we also not include Barnabas as an apostle, even though he is not named one explicitly, and possibly even Jude or John Mark who wrote the gospel of Mark? When one considers the Acts narrative and gospel writers, the picture begins to emerge that there were many other apostles after the original 12.

The question we should be concerned with is this: If there is a continuance of the apostolic office, how much authority do they have and how do they help the Church? Scripture answers these questions in 2 Corinthians 10-12 where Paul gives a defense for his apostolic authority over the Corinthian Church. Paul asserts that he may not be an apostle to others, but he is definitely an apostle to the Corinthians because of his relationship to them because he evangelized them and worked hard to establish them in Christ. Paul continues in 2 Corinthians 10:15-16 - "Neither do we go beyond our limits by boasting of work done by others. Our hope is that, as your faith continues to grow, our sphere of activity among you will greatly expand, so that we can preach the gospel in the regions beyond you. For we do not want to boast about work already done in someone else's territory." These verses teach us that apostles operate in spheres of influence by relationship and Paul is the apostle to the Corinthians, but he may not be the apostle to other groups of Christians who do not know him. The letter of Romans was written as an apostolic introduction to the Church at Rome explaining his doctrine and purpose of his visit to them. Apostles have authority over groups of Christians by their relationship to those Christians.

Some who oppose the continuance of apostles today propose that apostles somehow have the same authority as the apostles who wrote Scripture. That is simply not true. No one in the New Apostolic Reformation movement would propose that modern day apostles are writing new commands or have apostolic authority over the whole Church. We promote the offices of apostle and prophet function within the context of networks of relating Christians for leadership, guidance, church discipline, church planting efforts, and equipping the saints. These are mutually beneficial and God-given governing offices that, when recognized and operational, bring God's best for His Church.

The next question we should answer is why does relating to apostles and prophets bring a benefit to the Church? Our answer is found in Ephesians 4:11-13. The answer is found in a Greek word used only once in Scripture in Ephesians 4:12, *katartismos*, or *equip*. The Greek word is used in the following ways in the Greek lexicon; align a broken bone, clean or mend a fishing net, or make complete that which is lacking. These uses of the Greek word teach us that apostles and prophets bring a healing and "aligning" dimension to the Church. They "mend the net" bringing unity to the Church and make our faith complete because of their leadership grace gifts that Jesus gave to the Church. I propose that when the evangelical Church embraces the apostolic and prophetic offices, then we can expect what was promised in Ephesians 4:11-13 to emerge: The revelation and expectation of Christians who are powerful, equipped to the work of the gospel, unified in faith, mature and full of the experiential knowledge of Jesus Christ. Though we have not spent much time explaining the prophetic office, we did show in the previous chapter that prophets were operating in the Acts narrative, and that prophets were diverse in terms of gender and the context of their ministries. This is a short explanation of why we should align with apostolic networks. For a more in-depth treatment, see Dr. Che Ahn's *Modern Day Apostles* and Dr. C. Peter Wagner's *Apostles and Prophets Today* books for more biblical research and a deeper apologetic into this subject matter.

To close this chapter, we should look at some of the marks of an apostle. Apostles do the following: work signs, wonders and miracles (2 Cor 12:12); discipline the Church (2 Cor 12:20, 1 Cor 1:10); plant churches; preach the gospel with power

(1 Cor 2:4); make decisions in councils (Acts 15); live Christ-like lives to follow by example (1 Corinthians 11:1); endure hardship on behalf of the Church fighting for its future (1 Tim 4:10); and apostles teach the Church (1 Cor 4:17).

CONNECT GROUP QUESTIONS

1 – What are your feelings about local churches being submitted to apostles and prophets in the context of relating church networks? What might be some the objections that evangelical Christians have about receiving the apostolic and prophetic offices?

2 – Looking back through Church History, one can see that the function of an apostle has been present with the emergence of Christian movements and denominations led by strong leaders like Martin Luther, John Wesley, and modern leaders like Che Ahn. Why is it important to acknowledge the title of apostle even if the function of an apostle is already operating in the person's life?

3 – Have you personally benefitted from the ministry of an apostle or prophet?

Chapter Six

THE SEVEN MOVERS OF CULTURE

Genesis 1:28 - "God blessed them and said to them, "Be fruitful and increase in number; fill the earth and subdue it. Rule over the fish in the sea and the birds in the sky and over every living creature that moves on the ground." - NIV

Matthew 28:18-20 - "Then Jesus came to them and said, "All authority in heaven and on earth has been given to me. Therefore, go and make disciples of all nations, baptizing them in the name of the Father and of the Son and of the Holy Spirit, and teaching them to obey everything I have commanded you. And surely, I am with you always, to the very end of the age." - NIV

Matthew 6:10 - "your kingdom come, your will be done, on earth as it is in heaven." - NIV

Sociologists have observed that civilizations are ordered around 7 "movers" that bring order to people groups and shape their common culture. From the time of recorded history up to the present day, aggregates of people produce these 7 common spheres of influence. These movers or spheres of society are Family, Religion, Government, Education, Economy, Arts, and Media (the propagation of information). The verses quoted above support what sociologists have observed. Humanity, created in God's image, has been given the mandate to rule, reign, and order the creation after God's image in us. In addition to this, Christians see the created order as being subjected to the Fall, but also being reconciled in Christ. Christians are the change agents who bring the knowledge of reconciliation in Christ to individuals and to God's creation as we preach the gospel, demonstrate God's nature and character, and use His wisdom to live life, helping the people around us. The gospel is not only good news on Sunday but is still good news on Monday. Our faith lives in the everyday and God has given each of us a life to live that is unique to us, so that He may receive glory and we may receive the rewards of being good disciples.

When we look at Matthew 6:10, we see Jesus teaching us to pray for God's kingdom to come. This is His authority to rule and reign, as well as the desires of God's heart, to be a reality on earth in the same way God is King and Potentate in heaven. God, being Creator of all things is not just interested in our religious life, He is has an interest in and an agenda for all life because He created all things. God has thoughts about everything encompassing the human experience and He wants those thoughts to be realities in the lives of people. Many Christians in the Western Church think with a dualistic worldview that comes to us from the Greek philosopher Plato. Plato promoted the theory that the spiritual/soul is immortal, perfect, and pure. He called this form. Plato then promoted the idea that the physical realm, or realm of the flesh, is inferior, corrupted, and weak. He called this matter. Since Western civilization stands on the foundation of Greco/Roman civilization, we inherited a worldview that divides the human experience into secular and spiritual. However, a Biblical worldview sees the whole world as God's creation that is good and is integrated with God at the center. The Biblical worldview has all life revolving around God. He is intimately involved with His creation, and He desires people to live all the areas of their lives in the context of knowing Him. This means there is no secular/spiritual divide. Monday is as sacred as Sunday. Work is worship. Worship to God is living a life that honors Him in every area of our lives: Family, Religion, Education, Government, Economy, Arts, and Media.

Christians with a Biblical worldview believe God has thoughts and an agenda for all the 7 movers of a society. Matthew 28:18-20 teaches us that Jesus has all authority in heaven and on earth and He commands us, the Church, to express that authority to "all nations." The Greek word for nations, ethnos, clearly implies that whole people groups would come to the knowledge of Christ and live under His authority, obeying Jesus through their knowledge of Him by the agency of His Church (the total sum of believers). Jesus plainly tells us to expand His authority, rule and reign, and expects us to be successful. Since whole people groups are ordered around the 7 movers of society, Christians within those societies will disciple their nations by influencing those 7 movers. When God's people become the ones who are influencing all the movers of a culture, then that culture grows into a "discipled" culture because a godly worldview becomes the norm.

Christians cannot impose their influence in the 7 movers of society by force or theocratic methods. To influence the 7 movers of culture, Christians will need to know God's heart for the people who are in those 7 movers. The authority of Christ is spiritual, not carnal. Though our faith lives in the everyday, we only have the authority of Christ when we know Him intimately and live out the strategies He gives us. Our authority is by relationship, not Law, so our influence in the 7 movers of society reflects the redemptive, merciful, good and loving Savior, Jesus Christ. We cannot be influencers for Christ and be in the flesh. This is why becoming a disciple of Christ, who has cultivated a deep relationship with Him first, is the prerequisite for societal change. The strategies of heaven to redeem the world only come by revelation.

This is great news for all Christians because each one of our lives has eternal glory and value. The businessperson, the mom, the artist, the tradesperson, the doctor, and the teacher all have a ministry from Jesus to influence society for Christ through whatever mover of society they touch. Ministry is not just service to the local church; ministry is a life lived to the glory of God. Christians should see the local church as a reconciling, healing and equipping center developing Christians who can influence the 7 movers of society that they may touch in their daily lives. The current view of the local church by most Christians is a transactional, consumer-based experience. For Christianity to be apostolic, it needs to change in drastic ways that start shifting society. The Church of the First Century radically transformed the Roman Empire and influenced the 7 movers of culture to the point where the Roman world became a Christian world. It's time to shift from customer service-based Sunday experiences to radical faith-filled discipleship which will once again empower the gospel of the kingdom to change culture and society.

CONNECT GROUP QUESTIONS

1 – What 7 movers of society does your life influence? (Family, Religion, Education, Economy, Government, Arts, Media)

2 – How do you see the world and how would God move through your life to bring the knowledge of Him to the people around you? Have you ever considered the gospel is more than individual saving faith, but encompasses bringing the knowledge of Christ to all areas of life?

3 – How has dualism affected the way you see the world? Do you have a secular life and sacred life, or does your faith in Christ live in every area of your life?

RESOURCES FOR FURTHER STUDY:

Chapter One
Dr. C. Peter Wagner, Dominion - *How Kingdom Action Can Change the World*

Chapter Two
Dr. Stan Newton, *Glorious Covenant*

Chapter Three
Bill Johnson - *When Heaven Invades Earth*

Chapter Four
Dr. C. Peter Wagner - *Your Spiritual Gifts Can Help Your Church Grow*

Chapter Five
Dr. Che Ahn - *Modern Day Apostles*

Chapter Six
Johnny Enlow - *Seven Mountain Mandate*
Rob Covell - *The Revelation of Hope*

Made in the USA
Las Vegas, NV
14 November 2021

34452148R00046